D1168348

Riding Westward

Riding Westward

Carl Phillips

Farrar, Straus and Giroux / *New York*

Farrar, Straus and Giroux
19 Union Square West, New York 10003

Distributed in Canada by Douglas & McIntyre Ltd.
Printed in the United States of America
First edition, 2006

Library of Congress Cataloging-in-Publication Data
Phillips, Carl, 1959–
    Riding westward / Carl Phillips.— 1st ed.
      p.   cm.
    ISBN-13: 978-0-374-25003-4 (alk. paper)
    ISBN-10: 0-374-25003-0 (alk. paper)
    I. Title.

  PS3566.H476R53 2006
  811′.54—dc22

                              2005052080

Designed by Jonathan D. Lippincott

www.fsgbooks.com

10 9 8 7 6 5 4 3 2 1

Contents

Which one's the mockingbird? which one's the world?

          —Randall Jarrell

Riding Westward

Erasure

Brindled, where what's left of the light finds him, he cowers
in front of me: one way, as I remember it, that a body
having grown accustomed to receiving punishment expresses

receipt, or a readiness for it, or—wild, bewildered—the desire to.

Above us, the usual branches lift unprophetically or not, depending:
now spears; now arrows. There's a kind of tenderness that makes
more tender

       all it touches. There's a need that ruins. Dark. The horse
comes closer. A smell to him like that of the earth when it's been
too long dry, drought-long, and the rain just starting, that first release, up,
that the earth gives up like a name meant to be kept secret, or as when
the memory of rescue has displaced the chance of it, unlooked-for, into

clearer view: like that exactly: oh he smells like the sweet wet earth, itself.

Bright World

—And it came to pass, that meaning faltered; came detached
unexpectedly from the place I'd made for it, years ago,
fixing it there, thinking it safe to turn away, therefore,
to forget—hadn't that made sense? And now everything
did, but differently: the wanting literally for nothing
for no good reason; the inability to feel remorse at having
cast (now over some, now others), aegis-like, though it
rescued no one, the body I'd all but grown used to waking
inside of and recognizing, instantly, correctly, as mine,
my body, given forth, withheld, shameless, merciless—
for crying shame. Like miniature versions of a lesser
gospel deemed, over time, apocryphal, or redundant—both,
maybe—until at last let go, the magnolia flowers went on
spilling themselves, each breaking open around, and then
apart from, its stem along a branch of stems and, not of
course in response, but as if so, the starlings lifting, unlifting,
the black flash of them in the light reminding me of what I'd
been told about the glamour of evil, in the light they were
like that, in the shadow they became the other part, about
resisting evil, as if resistance itself all this time had been
but shadow, could be found that easily . . . *What will you do?*
Is this how you're going to live now? sang the voice in my
head: singing, then silent—not as in desertion, but as
when the victim suddenly knows his torturer's face from
before, somewhere, and in the knowing is for a moment
distracted, has stopped struggling— And the heart gives in.

Torn Sash

To each his colors: mauve, and yellow. And

cruelty, at most, only what we thought it was:
perhaps not unnecessary—there's nothing
useless—cruelty as a means of understanding,
if not absolutely, then more forcefully than not
love's conditions—not clear,

                 but clearer. Stars,
but only if refracted first, reassembled into lit
beadwork, a net veiling the faceless water's
veiled face, what the waves, like a memory of

waves—like memory—keep at once refusing,
and never quite let go of . . . Let a silence be

configured around what hurts most; around
that, a style pitched subtly between distraction
and an indifference, cool, ambitious, by which
the events of story rise steadily,

                 now history,
soon a legend that—forever, it seems—both
revises itself and is itself revised: *They agreed
to swear to have remembered nothing—and this
was true, or it was for one of them, though to*

all appearances equally each forgave the other.

Falling

There's a meadow I can't stop coming back to, any
more than I can stop calling it a sacred grove—isn't
that what it was, once? A lot of resonance, trees asway
with declarations whose traced-on-the-air patterns
the grasses also traced, more subtly, below. As for
strangers: yes, and often, and—with few exceptions—
each desperate either to win back some kingdom he'd
lost, or to be, if only briefly, for once free of one. I did
what I could for them. They did—what they did . . . It was
as if we were rescuable, and worth rescuing, both, and
the gods had noticed this—it was as if there were gods—
and the sky meanwhile crowning every part of it, blue,
a blue crown . . . There's a meadow I still go back to. It's
just a meadow—with, sometimes, a stranger, passing
through, the occasional tenderness, a hand to my chest,
resting there, making me almost want to touch something,
someone back. I can feel all the wrecked birds—lying
huddled, slow-hearted, like so many stunned psalms,
against one another—start to stir inside me, their bits of
song giving way again to the usual questions: *Why not
stay awhile here forever?* and *Isn't this what you keep
coming for?* and *Is it?* I'm tired of their questions. *I'm
tired*, I say to them—as, with all the sluggishness at first
of doing a thing they'd forgotten how to do, or forgotten
to want to, or had only hoped to forget, they indifferently
open, spread wide their interrogative, gray wings—

Sea Glass

It's cold here, in the wind. Night fog. We can

leave, if you like. Moral landscapes, coming down
as usual to a foreground all agony, pursuant
joy, more agony, a lesson
                              insisting hypnotically,
grass-like, wave-like, ever on itself—
                                        this time,
it's not like that. The body is not an allegory—it
can't help that it looks like one, any more than
it can avoid not being able to stay. All along,
it was true: timing really
                              is everything. I've

loved this life. If it's one thing to have missed
the constellations for the stars themselves,
it's another, entirely,
                        to have never looked up.
Some mistakes, given time, don't seem mistakes—
I'm counting on that; others, though perhaps
a little bit still worth being sorry for,
                                        lose force,
we forget them mostly, or we say we have and,
almost, we surprise
                        ourselves, even—we mean

what we say: *It's cold here. It's dark. Follow me.*

The Way Back

When he takes it by the neck, where the head should be,
repositioning the body so the markings at the wings
face up,

      he does it with a gesture so absolute in its
refusal to give anything of feeling away, that it seems
at first like a brand of precision—his own brand—

and not indifference.
                Prairie hawk, he says, *or an owl,*
it's possible. He speaks like a man who knows at

least a couple of things, maybe more than that, so
when he says *No animal—a knife did this*, meaning
the missing head,

           I believe him, in that way that
the effort to believe should
                    count as believing. Maggots

negotiate what's left of it, making the feathers
move very slightly, as if in a wind,
                  a small wind . . .

The urge to make meaning again—of everything,
his gesture, the knife-work, the corrupted body,
the body

—rises inside of me: as if it were sexual,
that's how it feels, and then,

                like that, no less abruptly,

how it falls away. —When was I last this alone,
with anyone? He looks up at me in that half-looking-
just-above-and-

          to-the-left-of-me way that's probably
a habit of his and, scooping the bird up in both hands,
he brings it close to my face,

               closer, until it hurts to look
as much, almost, as it hurts not to. I can smell
the rot of it; I can see the bird,

              I can see his fingers
around the bird—tight, not too tight, gentle—I can

almost see to where what happens next has happened.

Radiance versus Ordinary Light

Meanwhile the sea moves uneasily, like a man who
suspects what the room reels with as he rises into it
is violation—his own: he touches the bruises at each
shoulder and, on his chest,
                       the larger bruise, star-shaped,
a flawed star, or hand, though he remembers no hands,
has tried—can't remember . . .
                         That kind of rhythm to it,
even to the roughest surf there's a rhythm findable,
which is why we keep coming here, to find it, or that's
what we say. We dive in and, as usual,
                       the swimming
feels like that swimming the mind does in the wake
of transgression, how the instinct to panic at first
slackens that much more quickly, if you don't
look back. Regret,
                 like pity, changes nothing really, we
say to ourselves and, less often, to each other, each time
swimming a bit farther,
                 leaving the shore the way
the water—in its own watered, of course, version
of semaphore—keeps leaving the subject out, flashing
Why should it matter now and *Why,*
                     why shouldn't it,
as the waves beat harder, hard against us, until that's
how we like it, I'll break your heart, break mine.

The Smell of Hay

If I speak of suffering,
I don't mean, this time, how it refines us,
I mean less its music than what is music-like
about it—a tendency to diminish to almost nothing, then
it swells back. The way memory can resemble steeple bells,
the play of them, the bell ropes having left
our hands. Or like snow resettling
inside a snow globe picked up, shaken,
set down. Then we shake it again. Lost excellence
is a different thing. Men who make

no exceptions. Men who, because they expect everywhere
hard surprises, have themselves grown hard—fazeable,
fazed by nothing. Touch, as a form of collision;
a belief in divinity as a form of nostalgia. Husk of a libretto
for the world as—I can say it now—I wanted it: a room
that swayed with rough courtship; my body not mine,
any more to ransom than to refuse. On the window's
glass where the larger moths had beaten
against it, a fine powder, a proof by morning I had only
to blow across. And it flew. It scattered.

Ocean

Is the voyage over? This, the lull I've come to expect
after smaller victories, stunning blows of defeat? Or is this
but respite? The water has stopped its shifting, the ship
follows suit— Aboard the ship, like a hand abandoning
one gesture for another as the mind directs it, so
as the captain commands them the sailors variously
settle or, lifting themselves free from their having settled,
they rise to an attention that proves obedience can be a form
of love. He passes among them like a brightness, like
what he is: a man for whom they'd do anything, they're
a theft in readiness, magnolia forced too soon open—
split signatures, so many bruises on a freakish branch,
nodding, windless—they obey him as if divinity were
but one of several irreversible truths about him that each

had swallowed. They believe what he believes, without
exception: *There's a courtesy to be found everywhere—*
worth finding, the slightest act, his removing the cross from
around his neck before fucking a stranger, a grace almost—
why not believe that, having watched him, having been
instructed to? *There's a life after death. Each comes*
back to the world transformed, not human—some lesser
animal. The captain has told them already he'll return
as a horse—and swiftly, steadily, they do imagine it:
the captain rearing, his raised hooves casting about at the air
before finding the earth again, crushing the grass each
sailor hopes desperately he'll come back as—has every
intention to—a field and powerless, the captain a horse
the field contains now, now doesn't, may never again . . .

Brocade

As when the vine, climbing,
twisting—
as if would strangle—

doesn't, instead
ends each time in proof
of how to end is—or can be—

to be transformed: blue flower,
and then a bugle; then a mouth gone
blue with having meant to swallow,

not spill, not like this, the names
escaping, the ground
shelving, almost as if with the kind

of tenderness that hovers
over scant acquaintance
as it comes undone, silently,

mutually, regret
nowhere figuring, or not any
longer as an emotion, more

the inverse of one, as gesture
is memory's inverse,
memory given the properties

briefly of a body when it passes upward
and as if unstoppably through a heaven
of air, now you steady me,

and now you don't, surface
as of a pond I've crossed
often, have laid my head against,

body of winter in whom
the limbs of the trees crack
like favor, cold

into which I speak because
I *can* speak, making distinctions
because between to know

and to understand
there is still a difference,
suffering-as-pleasure

is not the suffering that must
make keen again what
pleasure has blunted, which I

believe, we shall want
for nothing, I believe that too,
or almost, why shouldn't I say so,

some admit to flaw, some sway
inside it, sing softly,
the better to bring a far thing

near, they tell me,
I tell myself, I sing as I can,
softly, as I sway among them.

Stardust

The new life only looked new,
                                 and only at first.

Nor is the spirit—whatever that is—crushable; to be
crushed isn't one of the spirit's properties, is
what I mean. Nor is allegiance, though
I am a man who has said otherwise, and perhaps
meant it once,
                    or that was once the idea. I've had many
ideas,
        some I remember still, though brokenly, as I do
people: less the face than the set of a mouth, say,
in anger, or sharp release; less the voice
than the silences falling, settling around what,
by definition,
                    they can never include.
Love doesn't require forgiveness. It favors tact
over honesty—
                    A fistful of leaves, over none at all.

Dreamer.

Dreamer turning in the dark that you dream inside of.

The Lower Marshes

Maybe humility is what the reeds
                       are for, as I've been told;
and maybe humility really is a virtue I should be more
concerned about,
               weaving among the lost as I've woven
so long, I astonish no one now, raise no suspicion. —When
did the damned become this indifferent?
                       Never to harm,
nor be hurt by . . . As if to want a thing—to believe in it—
might be enough at last, could make it true, sacrifice included.
Always, there's a face that—could I but find it—I'd know
anywhere, I'd remember:
               the worst kind of lonely, foundering
in every part of him—
              I'd remember that, in the face especially.
Wasn't sacrifice all he wanted, or at least believed he did?
Haven't I been true?
            I've meant no harm; don't intend getting
hurt by. Only those who lack suspicion or, worse, refuse it
need be astonished if I weave, still, among the lost as I've long
so woven, like one of several,
              like a minor concern that matters,
somehow. Are the damned so different? How call humility
a virtue when it comes this easily? To bend when made to, as if
having been told: that's what
              the reeds do. It's what the lost are for.

Island

Sea lavender, in staggered flower—
As for the sea: like a truce meant to last
only until each party has fittingly dismissed its dead—that's
how still it was. And the mind, without
having at all wondered if it could,

                        or how, moved elsewhere,
to where nothing as I'd understood it, as I'd been
given to understand it, could help, because none of it—
the handling of light as a form of prosody, the body
as body, the soul as a lantern swung, swingable against
competing darknesses, *Who goes there?* and *Who
has not?*—none of it was true. There was no worse
or better part of me—

                    Like choosing which one to be forever
changed into: the invisible sycamore, in fullest leaf,
or the equally invisible horse tied slackly to it.
Not wish; being forced to choose—and the only mercy,
that the end will be swift, irrevocable, and at first look easy. I looked
at you.

Affliction

The raptor's face hovers
over my face. I've let risk sustain me
this far before. I raise one arm,
two arms; the bird circles—

Chance entirely, how our gestures
fall into something now and then mistakable
for rough pattern. I like chance.
I like how the markings
at his neck suggest the hand
of an amateur; as if someone had traced
uncertainly an outline
in rust around the shadow
of a pair of wings only half-through

unfurling—fixed there, as if by the outline itself,
in that position; the strangest scar. Other
differences between us include
my being able to hold in check
briefly all my usual will
to conquer, which in the raptor
is the will to survive—I cast it
elsewhere. When I do, an ability
to feel sorrow—I don't
know why—replaces it: to feel sorrow
for some other creature,

not the sorrow *of* it, which would be
compassion. The raptor
hovers over me,
as if lifted on an impossible
cross between steady updraft
and a sense of restraint—
tight circles, each one
higher than the last, farther from me,
though I can see his face still: I recognize it,

with what I think must look
almost like tenderness
from so far away.

Bow Down

I

As if he, too, could see the world,
just in front of us,
coming divided: those who step
routinely toward a dark that, mostly,
has seemed avoidable;

those who let them—

                World from which,

if for no other reason, then
out of pity, I should
look away.

Out of decency.

I should try, or should seem to have tried, or to be about to.

II

If I don't go to him, if I do nothing, if he comes to me first,
and then I follow: does it count as trespass? Should it?
If he bends aside the lower branches— If I pass unmarked

beneath them— If I look away, as if toward something
difficult, bright, and departing always, like the parts of
memory that, very briefly, flare as what is remembered grows

more far; if I look away, and he does—if I could do that—
where does the damage go to, if damage figures here, if
no one sees it—no, if no one looks at it, if my stroking his

hair back also figures, gently, if I shall miss him, if I do already,
broad strokes, consolation, though there is nothing to console
him for, nothing, why cry out, if the mud washes easily, if

the bruise eventually undoes itself, if somewhere a kindness
still counts as anything, let it count as kindness, why ruin it
by saying otherwise, why even speak of it, why speak at all?

III

Once, to ask
meant a small departure, and then
a larger one, shape of going—far,
away. As where the meadow led.
Red of switchgrass. A calf by the rope
toward slaughter.
Did that happen? Do you
wish it had? Why should the saints stand
apart from me, as if between us, suddenly,
they could see a difference? Questions fell
the way water did, off of—no,
away from your body as, sometimes,
I would still remember it: you
making of your hand now a fist,
now a dove, where it finds my chest—has
found it—and after, settling. The descent
was easy. It always is. It always
has been. Think twice, or don't. Given
the face of God in front of them, some
look away, others look once
and know a blindness
ever after. Will it have been worth it?
Was it? Wasn't it? Is it only a wind,
or my own voice, stuttering now
against me? *Bow down, inside*
the shadows here, and know a peace that leaves
elsewhere all human understanding of what,

earlier, peace looked like, it seems
to say. No. I say so. Saying it, as if
into a wind. No. As if into the shadow-work
that is all, I think, the body will have
meant—each time keeps meaning: canopy,
leaves above me, something that
almost I can see around, though
not through, the leaves
muttering, where a wind lets them, where a wind
makes them, *Come here, clipped bird,*
spattered stag whose flank the shaft entered
easily—come here. And forget. And sleep.

A Summer

The latest once-more-with-feeling-please
manifestation of letting go, cadence of wings
folding, unfolding, nights at the pier, nights

beneath it, boat-rower, finder of lost things,
bodies at sea, the body as itself a sea,
crossed wherever crossable, *makes me feel*

so much better about my self makes me
feel good, as by arrangement, as of arms
and legs, as for an altarpiece in the sand,

ritual resting as much in the details, *careful*,
easy, as in what we make of them, the eye, if
faltering, not failing quite, X for speak no more,

for love also, also his mark, *you'll forget me*
only when I say you can, a rosewater X at
each wrist in the style of rope-work, restraint,

release from it, slavery is dead, everyone
saying so, singing it, believing it, let them—
a lovely rumor. Then summer was over.

Swear-to-God

So much for the fanfare others call disaster. Sure,
a sameness, if not to the fruit, then to the flowers—little urns, white,
    wax-like—
that come first. Some confusion was understandable. Courage
can look like abandon. Can't it? The abandon that nerve
alone powers isn't exactly the more common despair-powered kind, now

is it? Broken gull. Broken egret. Broken gull. So much for the shore.
Not unsexual. What I admired most: that each error had been
a clean one. No moral charge to it. There were forces to blame, real ones,
should one wish to do so: the wind, erratic; a snow of storms. I for one
did not. Do I look like I was raised to make mistakes? I do not, I wasn't,

I don't regret them. As for history—quail scattering up into their
    characteristically
reluctant-seeming version of flight, versus what they stood for,
versus what they seemed to—I've had my thrill. The throat exposed—
this time, at my having said so. Cut it open. This time, nobody's going
    anywhere.
No one gets hurt.

After

A bell swings, in darkness.

                    Dark, like the bottom of the well
of childhood, up the steep walls of which I'd spend hours shouting
words like *anthracite, ginkgo*—over and over, each word falling
back to me, until it stayed, and was mine: yes, that dark. And yet—
though it's dark, in the darkness through which the bell swings

I can tell it's fall again, the usual fireless fire the leaves make
as they give themselves over, first from their branches, then
a second time when—crushable, as the diminished tend almost as
willingly, it seems, as instantly to become—they give way beneath
and around those of us who have places to go, still, and believe
in getting there.

                    A bell swings; then darkness. —Is dying like this?

The bells in my head swing their own heads, their difficult black clappers
for tongues swing against them in turn, like memory, which is a wave
hitting shore.

To a Legend

Stargazer lilies, marguerites. But you
must have dreamt that. The field is
clearer now than you've ever seen it—

founders, as it should. As it must.
And the light passes over it; of course
it does. Makes visible what wasn't:
deer scat; fox-run. Pocketknife: not

lost after all. You can leave any time.
*Stand up in the field Lie down in it
Come here* And you do what they

tell you to. Strangers. Your body
includes them, the way light includes
everything it passes over, briefly.
And briefly defines: now you're

the horse, now the snow that veils it,
now the wild signature that the horse
keeps making, startled, inside the snow;

and now its rider—untrained, uncertain,
both. And the horse somewhere
understanding this. Somewhere inside—

as a field continues, far, past the part
that's seen of it. Something at once
still and rampant, as across the field
of a coat-of-arms that any field, seen

from above, makes sometimes. Even
flowerless. Of course it does. Even
foxless, and strange. You can do what

you want, and no hand stopping you,
the field that clear, and you as alone,
inside it, as ever before. You making
your own small, inadvertent shadows

around the light as you fall through it.
As fall you must. Blue wrist over
shin over ankle. On a ground of stars.

Close Your Eyes

Waterfowl, lifting off water their feathered cargo;
and the water after—just after—trembling like
water of course, muscular, then like a half-held
belief not only that affliction trumps rescue,
but that it should finally—why not? All along
the shore, I considered the difference between
the body as announcement, merely, and as
instruction, and could not decide. As if that
urgency that had burned always around the need
to decide—about everything, and as if absolutely—
had at long last stopped its burning, or now burned
more dimly. Wasn't the salt air many things
besides salt? Hadn't it always been? Semen,
rogue lilac, late-flowering Scotch broom . . . *Just
as long as we get there, eventually*, wasn't
that it? Misunderstood intention; intentions
understood where, from the start, there were none.
Bleached driftwood. The exposed roots of
trees whose names I'd known once, some I
remembered still, for others I made names up,
some I couldn't decide. Some victories depend
proverbially on surprise; others—the bulk of them—
on flexibility, displayed fan-like in the face of
what might look at first like defeat, like a chance
gone missing. Remnant fog; the glittering shore—
like a life, or a version of it, that I'd grown so
used to, I'd forgotten it almost. I'd forgotten you.
Trust me. Trust me, the way one animal trusts another.

Shall Want for Nothing

They'd confused pleasure with the making of pleasure,
the way others mistake exactness of composition for
perfection, and call it art. They'd missed the difference
between self-reflection and penetration, *into* the self—
past that—they'd mixed it up. The sex between them:
it was like watching two people step together from a vast
forest into a small wood—

                                small, but more perilous for
its seeming at first easier to make one's way through,
as if that meant safety. Each saw in the other the broken
version of what he'd hoped, once, to find. Each saw in
himself the diminished version of the man he had been—
that the other had broken. They believed this, though
neither had said so, or would, ever. And the belief, as
usual, had been enough, had come to that place where
what we'd rather not have to believe gets transformed
into hard truth before settling neatly among those harder
truths that, in turn,

                            shape the bearer of them, as feathers
give to wings a shape neither false nor true. They agreed
that nothing was as it should have been between them—
as if, somehow, they weren't like the rest of us. Wasn't it
spring again, the smell of it lifting like music, and then
like any man lifting himself, wordlessly, slowly up again
from beneath another? How else should it have been?

In Waves

It is a shadow I break inside of,
then break again. Am I not reliable?
Bells-in-a-wind,

in storm: there are worse ways.
*Everywhere, the lives that leave you—you, who
let them*, sorrow sings to me. Also regret. Also

apology. Then—rock-a-bye—
they leave too.
We're alone again. Sometimes I think

we are what force and a capacity for
being forced not so much
must look like, as can, the one

thrown crossways over the other. *Give me. Give it
to me. Give it back.*
As when he passes in,

then out of me, as if would steer toward a nobler
falling—nobler, farther, were there
such a thing, what

that might look like. A crown, a lily, a boat
with which, in which to rest, cargo-like, in the clear
of winter, then stir again—ravished,

ravishing. Things that are damnable.
Things that are damned. Who says so?
Who wants for nothing?

As when he passed, that first time, his good hand
over me, over
my hand—and I was changed:

Tremble, he says. I tremble,
changed, before him. *Stop it*, he says, he

says slowly, he pulls me close to him, *Stop shaking*.

Plumage

Like defining beauty without apology.
Like arguing for it on moral grounds. To that extent—yes,
sexual. Touching my hand

but not taking it—on purpose,
I think—briefly a gesture I'd at best once been fond of
somewhere else, someone,

You should come to me again,
more often, you should come
when I say—

       I was nowhere I'd been before,
despite parts I recognized: the old cathedral they'd recently
elevated to basilica,

its copper roof,
the light when it fell on it falling
no differently—a glove,

a gauntlet—falling through a space
where sorrow
wasn't sorrow, it only looked like that, patient there, hawk-like

in its patience in the sorrow branches.

The Messenger

What is it you had meant to say? What had
I said?
    And the snow fell to the same as usual
transfigurational effect, making the world seem
not the world, very briefly, and then what it
always is again: just the world—changed,
changeable.
        What happens, I think, is we betray
ourselves first—our better selves, I'd have said once—
and the others after, as if that made knowing
what to call it somehow easier, meaning less
unkind.
        Why give it a name? What makes me
want to?
        There's a bell tower near here
I'd meant to show you, how there's still a music
hearable, despite the bell itself missing—lost,
or stolen, though it is difficult to steal a bell
so large, presumably,
                and a shame to lose one.
I'd meant to show you that.
             Wind enters and leaves
the tower like a thing that lives there—but nobody
lives there, no one, I keep meaning to say.

Turning West

Through a distance like that between writing *from* a life
and writing *for* one, the words skeined like smoke upward,
as in prayer at first—then outward, a banner across which
a crown of lit candles had been stitched by some
otherwise forgettable
        lost hand . . .

                      Blue silk, the stitches;
black the banner:

        Like one of those signs that give,
irrefutably, and none expecting it, the heft of truth to
what had been but rumor. Fields—more fields; horses
whose champions-put-to-pasture idleness fooled no one.
We do what we have to. We continued our journey.
Above me, the banner opens and furls, and opens.

Chivalry

On the best days, apologies aren't the same
as legal tender, to want a thing isn't enough,
and you know it: you must want it badly.
A stranger turns to you, says *Call the sea delphinium,*
a bruise coming into its own—blue
is blue, and it makes no sense
how entirely he's read your mind, as if the mind were instead
a battlement, or what's left of one, from something large, Greco-Roman, circa
when translation meant literally to be swept from the earth and given
fixture, permanence in the form of a star,

and he had scaled it. Time passes, like the kind of neighborhood you
have no doubt must once have included him, its swift, downward
transition making the vote to remove the church's beautifully preserved
        windows,
lest they be shattered, easy, unanimous,
it seems to mean a diminishment of faith somehow—though,
on reflection, you know it means that and it does not. You have
no illusions. When he's silent, it's as if he's remembering, with some
difficulty, a sexual position he once found preferable. When he speaks,
he'll speak of love.

Truce

Have struck the earth the requisite number of times, slowly,

with the flat of my hand, have taken pains, muzzled the wilder dogs
into relative silence, have muffled all bells—

> Leaves. The light.
The trees filling, emptying.

> *What stumbled from the room*
when you did? What takes its place?

> And the usual birds—of compromise,
of failure—scavenger birds, at rest briefly
on a wind's updraft.

> *If there was nowhere a holiness to it, all that time—*
If there is no holiness—

Why not say?

•

> And because pity makes
everything that it falls upon

> at once less attractive, the gods
withheld it from him, admiring instead
his brow, the particular burnish that despair—not yet consented to,
faced squarely—

> seemed to give to it, as they came
closer, as the birds, too,

> descended, more cautious at first, preferring

instinctively the higher branches to the very low ones.

Lost, but for a Few Still-Bright Details

Of the sea coming, sea-like,
in; and the ships coming with it; and the quartermaster
rocking,
       sweating beneath his orison of song,
              of signal—

And when that, too, was over:

When it was dark:

I lit a torch, I threw it,
into the dark,
it turned over and over again
upon itself—*if*,
over *when*, over *if*—itself a thronedom,
weightless, unresisted, subject
only to its own no-turning-back
momentum, into
the dark, making visible
briefly those bits of the world that
it passed over and,
as when the back of a hand we've been
struck about the head
and face by enough before
no longer surprises,
whatever the torch lit, in passing, remained
flinchless, fell without flinching
back, into the dark the torch
left behind it, a hand moving less

with mercy than with an elsewhere-bound
indifference to which no mercy was
attachable, nothing was, I could
see that now—not revelation but
recognition of what no veil from the start
had covered—the torch
moved steadily, at the speed
exactly of requiring nothing at last
but its own forward motion and the dark across and

through which it turned—exact,
steadily—unstoppable,
even when it vanished, into the dark, to vanish
is not the same as stopping, not belief, not the will to believe,
even you, not a thing could stop it.

Forecast

Betrayal, all along, will have been the least of it.
Some fall like empire—slowly, from the wild, more
unmappable borders inward, until reduced to history,
to the nothing from which, in the end,

                                        history's made;
and others, they fall with the dizzying swiftness of
one of those seized-in-the-night

                              kingdoms—chambers
awash with the blood of princelings, their spattered
crowns toys now in the conqueror's

                                    fine hands . . . As for
the common choice, the rote of exile that most call a life,
days on end spent muttering about loyalty, tattooing
the word *Who?* over one nipple, *Why?* just below the other,
foraging

                    shirtless among the animals or, worse, only
watching them pass—blind, but for instinct—beneath
the stooped cathedrals that the trees make in a storm
that—forever, it seems—looks permanent: No. Even
slaughter will have been better, I think,

                              than that.

The Cure

The tree stood dying—dying slowly, in the usual manner
of trees, slowly, but not without its clusters of spring leaves
taking shape again, already. The limbs that held them tossed,

shifted, the light fell as it does, through them, though it
sometimes looked as if the light were being shaken, as if
by the branches—the light, like leaves, had it been autumn,

scattering down: singly, in fistfuls. Nothing about it to do
with happiness, or glamour. Not sadness either. That much
I could see, finally. I could see, and want to see. The tree

was itself, its branches were branches, shaking, they shook
in the wind like possibility, like impatient escorts bored with
their own restlessness, like hooves in the wake of desire, in

the wake of the dream of it, and like the branches they were.
A sound in the branches like that of luck when it turns, or is
luck itself a fixed thing, around which I myself turn or don't,

I remember asking—meaning to ask. Where had I been, for
what felt like forever? Where was I? The tree was itself, and
dying; it resembled, with each scattering of light, all the more

persuasively the kind of argument that can at last let go of them,
all the lovely-enough particulars that, for a time, adorned it:
force is force. The tree was itself. The light fell here and there,

through it. Like history. No—history doesn't fall, we fall
through history, the tree is history, I remember thinking, trying
not to think it, as I lay exhausted down in its crippled shadow.

Native

Pretend there's a choice:
you don't have to speak to him. When you
do, you can call it a dream, then
make it one, governed largely by the reckless
why not of a man convinced that his life
is over—the part of it, anyway,
that resembles a sea to which
maybe you should have listened less, but
there—you've listened:

you've heard.
What changes that?
Now the body's a guttering candle,
now one of those letters you're forever braced—
feverish—to receive: heavy bond, the words
across it raised slightly, you can
touch them or not, the air itself seems
all but touchable,
everywhere a brightness
as of mother-of-pearl pulled
sword-and-scabbard-style through a shaft

of fire. Why explain? Candles,
letters—you don't have to explain
a thing to him. Not anymore. You've loved him
in the way mostly the acts of Christ
can't be accounted for,
he should believe that by now, hasn't it

been years? Has it? *You look*
stranded, you say to him slowly,
meaning both things: the initial despair,
and that knack the marooned
find eventually for shaping a life from
what's left—some berries, the wrecked ship
for kindling, a view of the sea
whose fault it's been. Has it, in fact,

all been dream? In his eyes, the possibilities
tilt, sway—a no-man's-land
between the wicked
and the merely fallen. For a moment it feels
as it felt, briefly, that first time.

Deepest, Where the Water Looks More Green

By then, the storm had passed us; it broke steadily
apart, like a truth whose rugged exterior belies
its stamina over time—now you see it,
and now you'd like to.
                        When it comes to desire,
I've tried measuring the difference between remembering
a man's eyes and, dimly, some memory of
having been seen by them,
                        what that felt like, and
what it felt like after.
                        About devotion: I've known it,
and I've seen what gets daily mistaken for it
but in the end
                won't count—doesn't—about that much,
I'm sure. What if difficulty turns out to have
all along been the point, and worth everything,
all the hurt it required of us?
                        I loved him
as once I loved my very self,
                        a stranger says to us,
and we look away, as from a loveliness cast brutally,
irreversibly, down from grace—we look away—it seems
almost as if, at first, there'd been no storm at all.

Translation

Stillness of a body that seizure has just finished visiting, has

passed through. The trees, I mean. Oranges. Figs, and lemons. I forget
the dream that I'd had beneath them, only that I'd had one.
I woke from it. Nothing anywhere lacked definition.
Like vision in pieces, scattered, and now reconnoitering. You asleep
beside me. This life as a mown field contained by wilderness,

the wilderness ringed in turn loosely by possibility
in the form of countless unchecked stands of pliant grasses
in a wind forever ready to stop blowing, though it doesn't, ever, it doesn't
seem to— I watched you sleeping. All was stillness. I watched

your eyes keep not unshutting. The rest would happen
once you'd opened them. Bluish moths, strawberries, blue flowers. The
    rest you know.

Break of Day

Though it came close, conquest never
quite began to describe it, and now
nothing does—to try to would mean having

somewhere to admit to vision being what,
more and more, it seems, a thing to be
panned for from the very wreckage

over which, for a time, vision skimmed, had
darted . . . Not conquest, more like pillaging:
the stripping of bodies, then the storming

of them, face up, face down, preference
mattering then, as now, apparently.
The year in the usual way unravels, leaves

fill the yard, you can see now the thickness
of vine that, all summer long, strangled
the pear tree, still strangles it, has grown

into the trunk in places—doesn't this, too,
count as intimacy, can't it—you can see
the stunted fruit hanging there useless,

unable to fall, so much work to be done,
and done with, why should you be
exceptional? Not conquest, but a kind of

joy at last, wasn't it, even if joy only
in its smaller, more common forms—
It had seemed enough, you say to yourself

as you might to a stranger and, a little sadly,
it seems that it was enough, though what
stirs now, inside you, isn't sadness but

sexual, you recognize it by its bracing
resemblance to those moments in any
long estrangement when—yes—even

you've been known to forget, almost,
how the end got started. Very briefly,
the forgetting stands—seems to—for late

affection, falling with all the casualness of
snow at first, of ruin in a land that was once
called Ruin as, imperceptibly, the curtain lifted.

Armed, Luminous

About sacrifice, I am not
so sure now. A river falls or rises
according to what leaves

or enters it.
But sacrifice is not the river. Compassion
is not what leaves. For what enters,

I have many names—I'd decide if I could,
if I were meant to. There's an instinct
that is rare but does occur in humans,

the ones who themselves feel
no different—it's any hour,
forgettable—as they turn toward the work

whose power will break them
eventually, and make their name.
I turn everywhere,

I see the shapes by which
a holiness declares itself more
and more, as if to be noticed

were all it wants of me. The body,
for example, in a cloud
of mayflies stalled briefly in a light

that passes: now the moon—
now the stars appearing, choir-like,
with a choir's tendency to make

the soloist at once seem lonelier,
and more complete. I'm not reckless.
I'd comply, if I could. In dream,

there's a choice: precious freight,
or the barge that carries it,
or the water without which a barge

can at first seem nothing. I choose the water,
I choose with a wisdom that looks effortless
because it is. It's that kind of dream.

Riding Westward

Any sunset, look at him: standing there,
like between his legs there's a horse
somehow, on either side of it a saddlebag
of loss, a pack of sorrow, and him Kid
Compromise his very own shoot-'em-up
tilt to the brim of his hat self, smirk to match,
all-for-love-if-it's-gotta-come-to-that half
swagger,
        half unintentional, I think, sashay.
The silver spurs at his ankles where maybe
the wings would be, if the gods still existed,
catch the light, lose it, as he stands in place,
scraping the dirt with his boots: lines, circles
that stop short, shapes that mean nothing—
no bull, not like that, but scraping shyly, like
a man who's forgotten that part of himself,
keeps forgetting, because what the fuck?

As he takes his hat off; as he lifts his head
like if right now he could be any animal he'd
choose coyote; as all the usual sunset colors
break over his face,
        he starts up singing again,
same as every night, same song: loneliness
by starlight, miles to go, lay me down by
the cool, etc.—that kind of song, the kind
you'll have heard before, sure, somewhere,
but where *was* that,
        the singer turning this

and that way, as if watching the song itself
—the words to the song—leave him, as he
lets each go, the wind carrying most of it,
some of the words, falling, settling into
instead that larger darkness, where the smaller

darknesses that our lives were lie softly down.

Acknowledgments

I thank the editors of the following publications, where these poems first
    appeared:

Boulevard: "Break of Day," "Sea Glass"

Callaloo: "The Cure," "The Way Back"

Colorado Review: "Armed, Luminous," "In Waves" (as "Sway a Little")

Columbia: "The Lower Marshes"

Electronic Poetry Review: "Close Your Eyes"

Field: "Bright World," "A Summer," "Translation," "Turning West"

The Kenyon Review: "Affliction," "Erasure," "Radiance versus Ordinary
    Light"

Kestrel: "Native"

Lyric: "Stardust," "To a Legend"

New England Review: "The Smell of Hay," "Swear-to-God"

The New Yorker: "Forecast," "Island," "The Messenger," "Torn Sash"

Parnassus: Poetry in Review: "Brocade"

Provincetown Arts: "Ocean"

Rivendell: "Chivalry" (as "Poetry")

Salmagundi: "After," "Deepest, Where the Water Looks More Green"

Slate: "Riding Westward"

TriQuarterly: "Falling," "Lost, but for a Few Still-Bright Details,"
    "Plumage"

Underwood: A Broadside Anthology: "Truce"

Vespertine: "Shall Want for Nothing"

The Yale Review: "Bow Down"

"Bright World" also appeared in *Pushcart Prize XXX: Best of the Small
    Presses*, Bill Henderson (ed.), Pushcart Press, Wainscott, NY, 2005.

"Bow Down" received the 2005 Smart Family Foundation Prize from *The
    Yale Review*.

•

"The Smell of Hay": the phrase "lost excellence" comes from Thomas
    Merton's book *Thoughts in Solitude*, Farrar, Straus and Giroux,
    New York, 1956.

"The Lower Marshes": for the reed as symbolic of humility, see Dante's *Pur-
    gatorio*, Canto I.

The epigraph is from "The Mockingbird," Randall Jarrell, *The Complete
    Poems*, Farrar, Straus and Giroux, New York, 1969.